Going Green on the Inside

Compiled and written by Caroline Proctor

Get ready for a journey

Not very easy to say……

But will one day make this place an easier place to stay!

**Please grab a chance to make things new…
To spread the joy of a new idea that has in the
end worked for you…………..**

Going Green on the Inside
© Caroline Proctor

National Library of Australia Cataloguing-in-Publication entry

Author: Proctor, Caroline, author.

Title: Going Green on the Inside / Caroline Proctor
                .
ISBN: 9780992566708 (paperback)

Subjects: Health.
                Health attitudes.
                Organic living.
                Sustainable living.

Dewey Number: 613

Published with the assistance by www.inhousepublishing.com.au

The Philosophy...... *A new beginning*

As one moves along in life we start to see all creation as one, our similarities and our differences.
We are all made of the same goods.
Love is inside us all to find and experience differently, and each one of us expresses it to varying degrees.

If you let yourself slide into this knowing that we are really all the same, just different colors, shapes and personalities, you start to become more sensitive to how others feel.
This can then extend to our animal friends...............

It becomes harder to consume our little brothers and sisters who live along side us, who cannot speak up for Themselves.
They also cry in pain just like we as humans do.
They live alongside us and most of us love them.

It's been my journey to recognize, along with thousands of others in the world, that it certainly is not necessary nor even necessarily healthy to be a meat eater.

Why do we need to eat animal products when there are so many different choices available to us?
There are certainly lots of healthy choices from grains, legumes and vegetables.

Excursions to abattoirs......!

When I was around 12 years of age, I was taken on a school excursion to the abattoir!
Yes, and to this day I have still heard of children at ages of 10 being taken!
I suppose it's one way of teaching children what they are really eating as it is thought they are old enough to understand and accept this as a good reality? How can this be?
It made me wonder what sort of planet we are living on.
 Could this really be happening...?

I became a young vegetarian following the excursion.
A cousin of mine also at age 7 turned vegetarian following his school excursion to the abattoir.
I was the only vegetarian with another friend of mine following that experience.

Yes, when that happened that began my course of a new way of looking at life around me, especially our poor animal folk who wind up in the abattoir.
I was totally horrified.
I think the children today have become immune to stopping the meat eating as the force of habit has taken over, and it's out of sight out of mind.

A Change in Attitude……

Certainly a fair number of our population have sensitized to see the dreadful state and status of our animal children.

Whether you are a vegetarian for physical, (health) spiritual, or emotional reasons, it has come a time where being vegetarian is certainly spreading.
People are asking why others are continuing to eat meat and animal products.

It is a large split in the way we order and take care of our lives and the lives of others and even our children.
It is a way of uniting our thoughts with our deeds.
For example-many people love animals so much, work in animal shelters, have pets and lots of them.
Still cannot see that other animals deserve also to be unharmed, left alone to live out their lives, alongside us as friends.
In truth are our pets really different to other animals that are part of our dinner each night?
Therefore if we love our pets, follow this love to all animals, and so no harm by consummation of them.

All Animals are Equal......

This attitude is now extending to all animals to see them all not different to our pets.

With films that are popular like "Chicken Run" and "Charlotte's Web", and others, it is becoming clear that animal rights have started to have recognition.

People are grasping that animals have a plight, and feel upset by the cruelty and violence that they endure.

Action stems from our thoughts, so if this could be taken one step further, a unity of our thoughts, words and deeds, we would none of us eat meat, and feel a whole lot more united and powerful inside ourselves.

It is almost like quitting a bad habit where slowly given up it is suddenly gone.

If we all did this it would surely make the world a better place.

Many values would stem from this as a new experience for us.

We Have Enough......

Perhaps we could call this the coming Golden Age that has been spoken about, the values of non –violence.

Waiting for someone to come and change us, where we have the ability to awaken our own strengths if we work on ourselves-our own true spirit and its sense of non-violence.

We have lands that ARE plentiful in rice, fruits, and a large amount of grains. No shortage in our shops.

What more do we really need.

While such good foods are here for us, do we really need to eat meat and other animal products?

The fruit shops are a colorful and vast experience of abundance for health.

The butcher shops are certainly a different experience and again represent an unnecessary display of what we could do without.

As so many people are realizing, animals haven't come just for us to feed on, rather they are part of nature's cycle of existence for all our survival and do exhibit love as part of their growth on the planet as we do as humans.

All animals are our pets......

So many people know and have come to understand love for animals.

They exhibit this with their pets such as chickens, rabbits, Guinea pigs, cows and horses.

Especially the household dogs and cats have become like members of the family and are so well cared for...

People have now begun to value the animal world by paying for their medical care, (at times more expensive than for man himself).

In addition donating for animal causes with animal shelters and hospitals.

So one more step has been taken by many, to look at his the dinner plate and what is on it!

The logic is hard to understand why we still have Christmas turkey on our plates for religious festivals.

To those more sensitive to the animal plight it seems sad to see an animal on the plate especially for a celebration

To a vegetarian, the two simply don't go together!

Non Violence......

The Brahmins of India taught "ahimsa", meaning non-violence, and so the avoidance of meat eating.

They made the cow a sacred animal...and eat vegetarian food because of their religious beliefs.

The life of sacrifice a cow lives, giving of its milk for not only its children, is also an amazing example of sacrifice.

We all know that animals such as the cow, live a life of general peace and harmony, grazing and rearing their young.

They have advanced nervous systems as we do, struggle for their lives when attacked, and fight for their survival just as we would.

Even for the non-religious, it is surely simpler and pain free for all not to have to go through this process.

Since a lot of animals die in fear and pain, a lot of religions and wise say we in fact absorb these vibrations into our systems.

-you are what you eat- ancient wisdom speaking to our hearts.

This is not to be negative but to help one feel happier, purer, and uplifted in daily emotions and feelings.

Freedom from the karma of meat……

We seem to understand on a daily basis that what we do has effects.

Each action has a consequence we can usually see but is not always so obvious. If we think of all the actions that took place prior to having a meat dinner, it may make people think twice about having it as part of their meal; the negative actions that led to the produce being on our plates we must be digesting.

The heavy sadness or energy of the animal goes into our system.

Many religious and mainstream people are aware of the so called vibrations that go with this and for their own peace and happiness in mind, abstain from this.

To put it blatantly we don't want our stomachs to be graveyards.

One cannot help think that not eating meat is a good deed, so why not be the best you can while you're alive

Would people really want meat if they had to get it themselves?

Empowering yourself with a new diet......

As you enter a new world in becoming a vegetarian or even a vegan, its crucial to add a new and exciting menu to your day.
The products I have discovered have mainly come via the local health food shop.

These include the amazing-

1. Chia seeds.
These seeds can be mixed in water to make a very refreshing gel.
I drink at least 1 to 3 cups a day of chia seeds and find it so strengthening.
It covers my diet for a lot of essentials such as iron, magnesium and the omegas.
It's just so digestible in gel form.
It can be added to cakes and any recipe for added food value. (Great for growing kids).
I feel so grateful that I discovered the Chia seeds so easily digested and I know I am getting protein I need.
After being vegetarian for over 20 years, with the blood type they say that needs meat, I have found I am managing well especially since these new products have been introduced.

2. Seaweeds

Another amazing food I have come across is seaweed.

You can get the sticks and flakes of Kombu or Wakame at health food shops.

It's a great and natural way to flavour soups, mix in water, put in salads, and simply nibble on small pieces for a snack.

So amazingly unique to include in your diet.

Apparently it's one of the highest forms of calcium for us.

Certified Organic Wakame leaf (Sea Power) is one favorite.

Not only do you reap the benefits of the alkalizing effects of the seaweed full of vitamins and minerals, but you also become a vehicle to help raise money for the

Sea Shepherd Conservation Society.....

You become part of the energetic and devoted crusaders for our glorious sea brothers and sisters-the dolphins, whales, seals and others.

What a great way to help make a difference as a percentage of Sea Power profits are donated to the Sea Shepherd Conservation.

Daily Focus on Self Change......

If you can focus in your daily life in total concentration on what you say yes and no to, it allows you to easily shift in the transformation to become a vegetarian.

In each moment you have a conscious choice of how to direct your diet.

If you connect to each choice you make, and do it with awareness, before you know it, you will have become vegetarian.

So many say I would love to be a vegetarian, but I can't do it.

Being a process of change it takes time before the habits and desires to eat meat are truly gone from your mind.

Till the programming inside your mind has been undone.

I liken it to a computer.......whilst typing you have to stop and consider each word, consider each bite of food!

We have to stop and consider each individual action - and in no time you will realize you have survived a meal, a day, a week, a month, and you have not needed to consume meat.

It used to feel like I had won a challenge, akin to that of exercising or helping someone that made me feel good inside.

An easy way to contribute to making the world a more gentle place to be in.

The children......

All of us have passed through kindergarten, where the role of animals plays a very important one. Story books are full of real and imaginative detail about our animal friends.

If truth be known we have no books written about their destiny for becoming our food –the truth hidden in shame and discomfort.

For our children to know about this could damage the sense of beauty that is growing inside them, and the belief in guarding all our life resources on the planet earth.

It has come to my knowledge that the children generally have not been told the truth of what they are truly consuming in their lunches!

It is simply a no go there subject…

Many businesses and educational settings for children are beginning to acknowledge our need to "exist as part of nature."

This now needs to include the animals on the continuum.

It is our national hope now for a calmer and more respectful relationship to nature, and a strong motivation to be more aware in future generations.

If this is really the truth, we need to include the sustainability of ALL living animals and teach our children to not destroy living creatures for our food!

Vegetarianism is definitely integral to the green approach.

A Day as a Vegetarian......is easy

To actually live a vegetarian lifestyle **is** not as challenging as it sounds.

The day can begin with a hot drink, followed by a bowl of cereal, or a power food as oats; to make this an even fuller meal you can add cinnamon, yoghourt, dried fruits, and eat citrus following

This sort of breakfast goes a long way-the oats draw out bad fats and have numerous benefits of being a long lasting food made to last the distance till lunchtime if necessary.

Snacking on fruit, nuts and dried fruit is always filling and energizing in between meals.

When its lunchtime it's time to grab sandwiches…

There are so many sorts one can consider with salads, cheeses, nut spreads, really endless combinations.

When it finally gets to dinner it's easy to substitute meat with tofu, beans, nuts-either combined with grains-rice or pastas and vegetables.

The combinations are again endless.

Indian dahls and rice, noodle dishes with tofu make delicious meals.

Breakfast Focus......

To start with a breakfast that's right for just you, is really the most important factor.....

What is recommended by others can simply not work for you, so it is really necessary to try different menus till the right one feels best giving YOU the most energy and wellbeing.

Some mornings we may not be hungry at all-that may be okay unless it brings on headaches later from not enough food energy in your system bringing on low blood sugars.

To start with a warm drink such as a green tea or a coffee may be ideal. For those more health oriented to alkalize your system with a drink of water and spoon of lemon juice is best (or an aloe vera juice of your choice at the health food shop).

Another great health choice is also organic cocoa, to make a hot chocolate; in Ayurvedic cooking from India this is said to be one of the most amazing food sources.

Another option is to have a glass of spirulina or wheat grass juice followed by a citrus fruit-orange is great.

This serves to double your iron and B12!

Lunch Focus......

We all need a good solid lunch to keep us going.

It's an easy focus to find that alternative filling to meat in your sandwiches.

Falafel balls are great cut up, then there is tahini-dark or light, full of calcium made of sesame seeds.

If it's the true Aussie flavour you need you can always use vegemite or have a toasted cheese and tomato...

Salad by itself or with cheese, if you're not yet a vegan!

Following the Indian menu is wonderful, having a dahl lentils or other bean choice and rice, with a touch of yoghourt to make a full protein.

The choices are endless and there is truly so much choice as a vegetarian that make it easy to get by.

Delicious and nutritious lunches happen easily when a good and wholesome bread is chosen.

There are so many wonderful grain breads available at the health food shops to choose from, and now even at supermarket and some fruit shops.

The combination of a grain and legume (even fresh alfalfa) produces protein.

The Middle Eastern falafels produce this with the combinations of exactly that – grain and legume as the falafel balls are chick pea.

So enjoy a vast choice for lunch and have great energy.

Your friends of all ages will be grabbing for your amazingly fresh and healthy lunches.

Dinner focus......

To have a beautiful and heartwarming dinner as a Vegetarian is an easy task.

Depending on the season you may prefer hot foods in winter - heartwarming soups with lentil, or any bean of your choice.

You can add vegetables and rice or keep it simple depending on what your tastes are. The substitute for meat can be tofu, which can be cooked in so many ways to make it what you want it to be.

It's easy to cook up and add a soya sauce or fry it to taste with herbs.it feels so light and easy to digest but it also gives you the feeling of a protein, very sustaining.

The choice of all the legumes which can be so richly cooked also give that sense of fullness from the protein. With pastas and rice dishes there is so much variety all to form a great dinner.

The many new vegan and vegetarian restaurants around show how creative it can be, leaving a feeling of lightness on the digestive system rather than sluggishness.

Pizza also is an easy alternative where now there are always Vegetarian ones on board the menu....when eating out.

If the energy and time is put into the food it will be enjoyable. In our fast moving day we now have so many good wholefood places where you can get healthy vegetarian food on the run.

Quotes of the famous and not so famous…...

"For as long as men massacre animals, they will kill each other. Indeed he who sows the seed of murder and pain cannot reap joy and love." (Pythagoras)

"Vegetarian isn't a diet it's a way of life" (Raam Proctor)

"There is a history of blood and tears from the animal that we can do without, let alone need to create and pass on to our children…." (Caroline Proctor)

"Since visiting the abattoirs of the south of France, I have stopped eating meat." (Vincent Van Gough)

"To become a vegetarian is to step into the stream which leads to Nirvana." (Buddha)

"The greatness of a nation can be judged by the way its' animals are treated" (Mahatma Gandhi)

'Nothing will benefit human health and increase chances for survival of life on earth as much as the evolution to a vegetarian diet." (Albert Einstein)

Vegetarian Shopping List……

There are so many wonderful products in the super markets' vegetarian sections and health food shops.
Let's make a list so you can add to your cupboard to slowly become meat free.
Not all the products are liked by all, but you just have to find the ones that agree with you that you can chop and change according to your bodies' reactions and desire.
You can buy the products ready made to add to your dinner plate or to add as ingredients to your cooking instead of meat.

1. **Baked beans (Supermarket or other)**
2. **Tahini (dark or light)**
3. **Tofu (all sorts spiced and not spiced)**
4. **Nimbin Cheese (no animal rennet)**
5. **Vegetarian sausages and other imitation meats (supermarkets)**
6, **Red Lentils (chick peas, brown lentils and all other beans (to add to vegetable soups or cook as Indian dahls) (Indian grocery shops and supermarkets) canned or fresh for cooking.**
7. **Chia seeds (local health food)**
8. **Falafel balls (Yumis falafel packs-gluten/wheat and dairy free-local supermarkets)**
9. **Wakame Seaweed (Health food shops)**
10. **Nuts of all sorts-almond and cashew….-protein**
11. **Humus dips for protein**
12. **Spirulina(local health food shops)B12.**

Vegetarianism and Spirituality......

Being a vegetarian is certainly linked in a marriage with the Spiritual Path.....

It connects all actions towards a path of non–violence inner peace.
Just to know that what you're eating has come from peace and love, not killing, makes the diet like a sacred act.
When I became a vegetarian, I knew that each time I ate, I was making a special confirmation to my own belief system of non-violence and peace, to make the world a more beautiful place to live in.
It came to my attention, that in this simple choice I made, I was creating a feeling of evolving my own soul towards its destiny by unity of thought, word, and deed that is so empowering...
My thoughts, words, and actions became one.

This all seems linked in a major way to the Golden Age and Earth Ascension that has already quietly begun.
It's been contemplated and announced by various Spiritual Leaders, and this I believe is part the world's new journey to be non-meat eating, and eventually vegan.

The Dreams of the Animals......

Many years ago, I had dreams which always seemed to include animals in them.....
Over the years I had forgotten all about these.
In 2014 I suddenly remembered these dreams which had been forgotten by me........and realised something major.
The animals were trying to get me to hear them....how Incredible..........
My most potent and emotional animal dream, came in a country house setting....
I was inside, when suddenly, looking out the windows, I saw lots of cattle. They all began to try to knock the walls down by taking running aims at the window areas.

I remember feeling so distressed in these dreams, as this Theme continually came into my dream world.
At the time I was a vegetarian already, and still felt most uneasy inside myself that the rest of the world was not!!
How could this be going on?
The animals showed me, which I only realised in recent times, that by these dreams they needed a voice and were outraged.
I now understand that this chaos in my dreams represented the Animals' efforts to express themselves to me, knowing I had become vegetarian was not enough as all need to be for them to be finally be left alone and at peace.

New Doorways as Vegetarian......

To finally recharge yourself, your life and emotional battery-going green on the inside, leaving meat behind can be one of the most important positive life decisions and commitments you can make.

More love, peace, truth, non-violence, and righteousness grows like a flower.

It's my belief that it leads to a chain effect of goodness to spread to others.

Many new doorways open to a new way for the future for our children and for planet earth.

To stand in integrity regarding our diets is so important.

There are so many efforts to help improve and better the earth, this is one achievable effort that can we can make to start to work on our own selves and our contribution to mother earth.

May your journey to becoming a vegetarian open up a whole new way of thinking and positivity as it has for me and many others. Please feel free to email any questions.

May your vegetarian journey begin!

(Caroline Proctor)

caaz@optusnet.com.au